Olympic Greats

OLYMPIC SWIMMING AND DIVING LEGENDS

MARTIN GITLIN

BLACK
RABBIT
BOOKS

Bolt is published by Black Rabbit Books
P.O. Box 3263, Mankato, Minnesota, 56002.
www.blackrabbitbooks.com
Copyright © 2021 Black Rabbit Books

Jen Besel, editor; Catherine Cates, designer;
Omay Ayres, photo researcher

Library of Congress Cataloging-in-Publication Data
Names: Gitlin, Martin, author.
Title: Olympic swimming and diving legends / by Martin Gitlin.
Other titles: Swimming & diving legends | Bolt (North Mankato, Minn.)
Description: Mankato, Minnesota : Bolt is published by Black Rabbit Books,
2021. | Series: Bolt. Olympic greats | Includes webography. | Includes
bibliographical references and index. | Audience: Ages 8-12 years |
Audience: Grades 4-6 | Summary: "Meet some of history's greatest Olympic
swimmers and divers, and explore their incredible careers"– Provided by
publisher. Identifiers: LCCN 2019028402 (print) | LCCN 2019028403 (ebook) |
ISBN 9781623102678 (Hardcover) | ISBN 9781644663639 (Paperback) |
ISBN 9781623103613 (eBook) Subjects: LCSH: Swimming–Records. | Diving–
Records. | Swimmers–Rating of–Juvenile literature. | Divers–Rating of–Juvenile
literature. | Olympic athletes–Juvenile literature. | Olympics–History–Juvenile
literature. Classification: LCC GV838.5 .G58 2021 (print) | LCC GV838.5 (ebook) |
DDC 797.2/1–dc23
LC record available at https://lccn.loc.gov/2019028402
LC ebook record available at https://lccn.loc.gov/2019028403

Printed in the United States. 2/20

All statistics are through the 2016 Olympic Games.

Image Credits

CONTENTS

Amazing

ATHLETES

They glide through the water. They dive from amazing heights. Swimmers and divers are amazing athletes. The world's best compete in the Summer Olympics.

The Summer Games are held every four years. Countries send their best athletes to compete. They splash up some great action.

Powerful SWIMMERS

Matt Biondi

Matt Biondi went to three Olympics.

He really shined in the 1988 Games.

Biondi **dominated** the freestyle races.

He medaled in four **individual** events.

He helped Team USA win three **relays**.

He also set three Olympic records.

COUNTRY	UNITED STATES
OLYMPIC YEARS	1984, 1988, 1992

BRONZE MEDALS	SILVER MEDALS	GOLD MEDALS
1	2	8

OLYMPIC SWIMMING EVENTS

There are 17 different men's swimming events. There are 17 for women too. Each event uses one or many of these strokes.

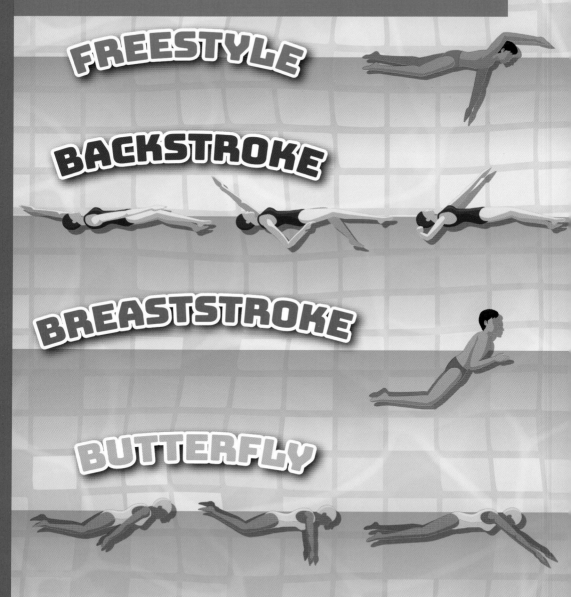

FREESTYLE

BACKSTROKE

BREASTSTROKE

BUTTERFLY

Krisztina Egerszegi

Krisztina Egerszegi was an amazing backstroke swimmer. Beating her was nearly impossible. She won the 200-meter backstroke event in 1988, 1992, and 1996. She was also a powerful **medley** swimmer.

COUNTRY
HUNGARY

BRONZE
MEDALS
1

GOLD
MEDALS
5

1988,
1992, 1996
OLYMPIC YEARS

1
SILVER
MEDALS

She is the first female swimmer to win five individual gold medals.

Ender's
World Records at the 1976 Games

100-meter freestyle
55.65 seconds

200-meter freestyle
1 minute, 59.26 seconds

100-meter butterfly
1 minute, 0.13 seconds

Kornelia Ender

Kornelia Ender was the youngest woman to win eight medals. She earned three silvers at age 13! Four years later, she won three individual golds. This amazing swimmer also helped her relay teams win two medals.

COUNTRY EAST GERMANY*

OLYMPIC YEARS 1972, 1976

BRONZE MEDALS	SILVER MEDALS	GOLD MEDALS
0	4	4

*East Germany is a country that no longer exists.

Greg Louganis

This dynamite diver won silver at age 16. He was just starting to show his **talent**. Greg Louganis went on to win two events in 1984. He won them again four years later.

COUNTRY   UNITED STATES

OLYMPIC YEARS   1976, 1984, 1988

BRONZE MEDALS   0   SILVER MEDALS   1   GOLD MEDALS   4

Louganis hit his head on the board during
the 1988 Games. That ruined his dive.
But divers get more than one try.
He came back to win gold.

Kristin Otto

Kristin Otto competed in just one
Olympics. That was all she needed.
Otto entered six events. She took gold
in all of them!

COUNTRY
EAST
GERMANY

BRONZE
MEDALS
0

GOLD
MEDALS
6

1988
OLYMPIC YEARS

0
SILVER
MEDALS

Otto won many different events. She won two individual freestyle races. She also won in backstroke and butterfly races. Otto even helped her team win two relays.

FUN FACTS

HIGH DIVE PLATFORMS ARE ABOUT **32 FEET (10 M)** HIGH.

Men's swimming became an Olympic sport in 1908. Women's events were added in 1912.

Olympic pools must be between **77 AND 82 DEGREES FAHRENHEIT** (25 and 28 degrees Celsius).

Michael Phelps

Michael Phelps is the greatest swimmer of all time. He earned 23 gold medals. No other swimmer has won close to that many.

Phelps was focused and **driven** to win. He was also built for success. His long arms helped him power through the water.

COUNTRY UNITED STATES

OLYMPIC YEARS 2000, 2004, 2008, 2012, 2016

BRONZE MEDALS 2   SILVER MEDALS 3   GOLD MEDALS 23

PHELPS'
OLYMPIC RECORDS

As of the 2016
Games, he held
speed records
for seven
Olympic events.

200-METER FREESTYLE

200-METER BUTTERFLY

200-METER MEDLEY

400-METER MEDLEY

100-METER FREESTYLE RELAY

200-METER FREESTYLE RELAY

100-METER MEDLEY RELAY

TOP CAREER GOLD MEDAL WINNERS IN OLYMPIC SWIMMING

Name	Medals
AMY VAN DYKEN (UNITED STATES)	6
KRISTIN OTTO (EAST GERMANY)	6
RYAN LOCHTE (UNITED STATES)	6
MATT BIONDI (UNITED STATES)	8
JENNY THOMPSON (UNITED STATES)	8
MARK SPITZ (UNITED STATES)	9
MICHAEL PHELPS (UNITED STATES)	23

MEDALS 0 4 8 12 16 20 24

Mark Spitz

Mark Spitz was the best Olympic swimmer for many years. In 1972, he won all seven of his events. He won all his individual butterfly and freestyle events. He also helped the U.S. team win three relays.

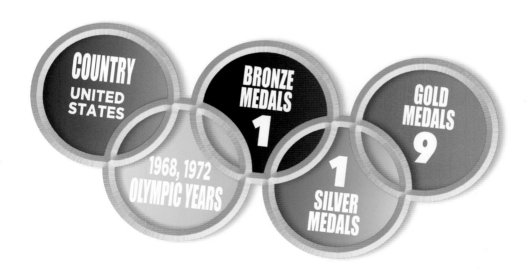

COUNTRY
UNITED STATES

BRONZE MEDALS
1

GOLD MEDALS
9

1968, 1972 OLYMPIC YEARS

1
SILVER MEDALS

Ian Thorpe

Ian Thorpe is among the best freestyle swimmers ever. He took gold twice in the 400-meter. He medaled in the 200-meter twice, as well. He also helped Australia medal in four freestyle relays.

COUNTRY **AUSTRALIA**

OLYMPIC YEARS **2000, 2004**

BRONZE MEDALS | SILVER MEDALS | GOLD MEDALS

1 | **3** | **5**

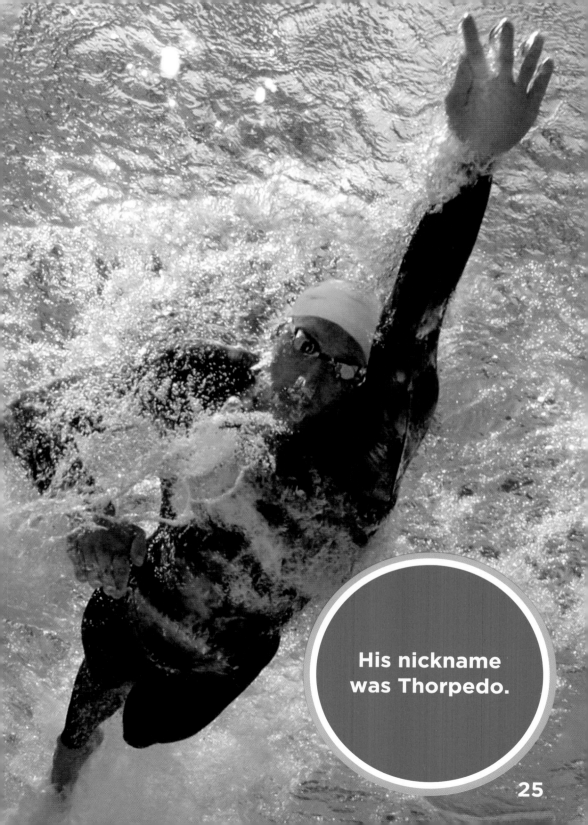

His nickname was Thorpedo.

Johnny Weissmuller

This super swimmer won five gold medals. Weissmuller earned three golds in individual freestyle events. He set Olympic records with each gold. He also helped his relay teams win two golds.

COUNTRY UNITED STATES

OLYMPIC YEARS 1924, 1928

BRONZE MEDALS 1

SILVER MEDALS 0

GOLD MEDALS 5

CHAPTER 3

Comparing

Swimmers and divers push to be

the best during the Summer Olympics.

Compare the stats of some of the best.

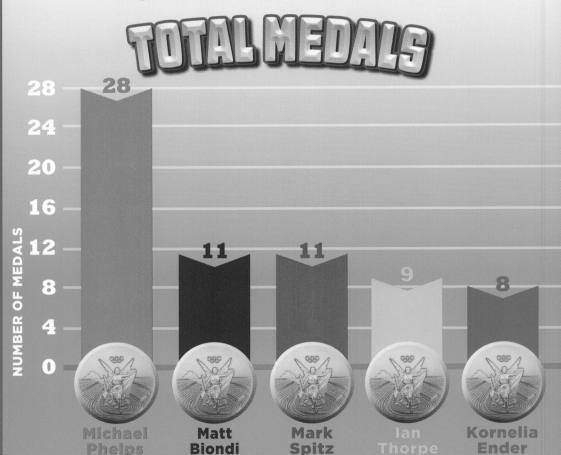

OLYMPIC APPEARANCES

Athlete	Number of Olympic Appearances
Kristin Otto	1
Kornelia Ender	2
Mark Spitz	2
Ian Thorpe	2
Johnny Weissmuller	2
Matt Biondi	3
Krisztina Egerszegi	3
Greg Louganis	3
Michael Phelps	5

NUMBER OF OLYMPIC APPEARANCES

0 1 2 3 4 5

7 — Krisztina Egerszegi

6 — Kristin Otto

6 — Johnny Weissmuller

5 — Greg Louganis

dominate (DOM-uh-neyt)—to hold a commanding position over

driven (DRIH-ven)—determined to succeed

individual (in-dih-VID-you-uhl)—meant for one person

medley (MED-lee)—in swimming it's the use of all strokes

relay (REE-lay)—a race between teams in which each team member successively covers a portion of the course

talent (TAH-lent)—a special ability for something

BOOKS

Allan, Morey. *Swimming and Diving.* Summer Olympic Sports. Mankato, MN: Amicus High Interest, 2016.

Fishman, Jon M. *Michael Phelps.* Sports All-Stars. Minneapolis: Lerner Publications, 2017.

Nussbaum, Ben. *Showdown: Olympics.* Huntington Beach, CA: Teacher Created Materials, 2019.

WEBSITES

Michael Phelps: Olympic Swimmer
www.ducksters.com/sports/michael_phelps.php

Olympics Coverage from SI Kids
www.sikids.com/olympics

Sports | List of Summer and Winter Olympic Sports
www.olympic.org/swimming

INDEX